Getting Rid Of Termite

The Best Approach To Control And Terminate Termite

Uriel Vick

Table of Contents

CHAPTER I

Description

A mite is a minute arachnid, usually measuring less than 1 mm in period. It belongs to the magnificence Arachnida and the subclass Acari. The arachnids are recognised for having jointed limbs and chitinous exoskeletons. Its subclass, Acari, consists of the mites and ticks.

Termites are social insects that stay in colonies. Each termite has a particular function within the colony. The queen lays the eggs - in all likelihood numerous thousand every day in a few varieties of termites. Workers termites are the best ones that cause harm to wooden - their activity is to accumulate meals and increase the colony. Soldiers have massive heads and long jaws they use to defend the colony from enemies. The termites that you could see are the winged reproductives that swarm in early spring.

One of a kind forms of termites

Yes, the three primary sorts of termites inside the United States are dampwood, drywood and subterranean. Dampwood termites commonly live in closely forested regions of the us of a as they opt for moist timber; at the same time as, drywood termites, a whole lot greater rare within the United States, choose extraordinarily dry wooden. Subterranean termites require moist environments, stay especially inside the soil and are the most destructive species.

CHAPTER II

Signs of Termite Infestation

Mud Tubes

Termites create dust tubes or mud tunnels as a way to without difficulty switch from soil to the wood of a shape. They move slowly via these in order that they will now not get dry out by means of the sun and air. Usually those mud tubes can be located on partitions, soils and dark places. Sometimes be determined on foundation walls in hidden, darkish places.

Wood Flooring Problems

Have you ever seen bubbles or bumps in your timber flooring? Well, that normally takes place due to water. However, this may be a sign of termite infestation and that's why you need to name Pest Control Company to come back and look into your private home.

Other timber damage

We all realize that termites devour wood to derive cellulose and electricity obviously. So, that is one of the most essential signal you need to vigilant approximately. Well, having this signal means you're already late in investigating the termite infestation at home, however nevertheless you may take some moves. Once you may discover the hallow sounds in any part of your property then you can without difficulty protect your own home from getting the state of affairs from your manipulate.

Clicking Sounds

When termites talk, they make clicking sound. When you are investigating your own home you then have to be cautious to listen such kind of sound. If you hear it then it's truly the time to name the experts.

These are the not unusual signs which you need to appearance out to realize your house in invaded by termites. But, other than these signs and symptoms there are a few different signs also that usually make people confuse with termite infestation.

Discarded wings

Both young male and female winged termites emerge from their nest to mate and find new area to invade different place most likely our houses in the springtime.

Their discarded wings within the home windows and close to doors is the primary sign of termite infestation, however you will want to know that ants additionally have wings which are frequently incorrect with winger termites. You should understand the simple distinction among ants and termites.

Preventing Termite Infestations

Make the Structure Less Attractive to Termites

While constructing you assets use the concrete foundation and go away ventilation area in between the timber and soil. Well, you may also name the expert pest manipulate technicians at this time as properly. They offer pre-production and submit creation termite control offerings which help you to maintain the termites faraway from your own home.

Maintain the Termite Prevention Features

☐ Make certain the soil round the foundation are dry. Keep it dry via right grading and drainage (which include the maintenance of gutters).

☐   Ensure there's establishing which can offer termite get entry to to the shape.

☐   Fix leaks straight away.

☐   Keep the vents from any kind of blockages, which includes plant life.

☐   Do not allow to develop your timber and shrubs towards uncovered wood surfaces. Or, do now not plant them neat the shape.

☐   Pile or save firewood at least 20 ft faraway from your private home.

☐   Inspect your private home periodically to ensure no termites colonies have mounted.

Limit the Termite Attractions

You need to be questioning what can really appeal to termites to your home. So, there are numerous matters that could give a cause to termites to invade your home. Here are the commonplace things which can make your home attractive to termites.

Moisture inside the wood

There are the generally 3 kinds of pests – Subterranean, Drywood and Dampwood. And dampwood termites entice closer to the timber that is water damaged or without delay rests on the earth. If you have got any sort of such wood near your private home or status water close to the source of woods then you are mistakenly inviting termites to your private home. Clearing the woods and by means of proscribing the moisture in the area you may decrease the possibilities of termite infestation.

Causes Of Termite

Lack Of Repair

The property which can be already harm draws termite the most. This is because it makes plenty less complicated for them to work on. So, maintain your home up to date. Make upkeep if needed to lessen the probabilities of termite infestation at your house.

No Normal Inspection

One of the most commonplace motive why termite infestation cross omitted is because of no everyday inspection of the property. You ought to investigate your house in regular basis due to the fact the faster you will observe something, the faster you could take moves to save you something actually huge from happening.

The most vital issue is to get rid of the conducive conditions termites want to continue to exist. Termites love moisture; keep away from moisture accumulation around the muse of your own home. Divert water away with well functioning downspouts, gutters and splash blocks. Reduce humidity in move slowly areas with right air flow. Prevent shrubs, vines and different plant life from developing over and protecting vents. Be certain to cast off vintage form forums, grade stakes, and so forth., left in area after the building changed into built. Remove old tree stumps and roots around and underneath the constructing. Most importantly, dispose of any wood contact with the soil. An 18-inch hole among the soil and wood portions of the constructing is ideal. It does not harm to automatically look into the muse of your private home for symptoms of termite harm.

Types of Termite Treatments

Non-Chemical Treatments

It's not important to use chemicals or pesticides or pesticides to do away with termites from your home. There are some methods through which you could keep termites far from your own home with out the utility of pesticides which can be as follows: –

☐ Physical barrier, commonly included during creation is one of the non-chemical remedies for termite manage.

☐ For physical obstacles – metallic mesh and sands of unique sizes had been proven powerful performance in controlling termite infestation.

Chemical Treatments

Before using any pesticide or insecticide the exterminator or pest manipulate specialists take a look at the pesticide to decide that it'll now not pose unreasonable risks to humans's health. Usually the exterminators called the pesticide as Termiticides which might be in particular designed to kill termites. And the application of these pesticide must be carried out by using a expert or trained pest control professional.

Approved treatments include:

☐   Building   materials impregnated with termiticides.

☐   Termite baits.

☐   Liquid   soil-carried   out termiticides.

☐   Wood remedies.

Termite Baits

There   are   numerous   bait structures   which   have   been introduced to assist in reducing the general use of insecticides and pesticides as this can have a bad effect on human's fitness and environment.

The most commonplace active components observed in termite baits are:

- ☐ Diflubenzuron
- ☐ Hexaflumuron
- ☐ Hydramethylnon
- ☐ Lufenuron
- ☐ Noviflumuron

The Safety of Pesticides Against Termites

The software of the pesticides will really damage the termites but there's also the chances of harming yourself at the same time as using it. So, the experts advocate to examine the commands carefully and also comply with the label guidelines. The product ought to meets modern-day safety standards to protect human fitness and the surroundings. Many pesticides which can be designed for killing termites are rather toxic, making it important to observe label directions with delivered care. Pest control experts have the know-how, knowledge, and all of the required gadget, which minimizes dangers and maximizes effectiveness. Hence, you should call the exceptional pest control business enterprise in Delhi NCR to do away with termites.

How to Handle Termite Infestation

Choose the Best Termite Control Expert

There are various things you could do for termite control and the great manner to remove termites is hiring expert pest control technicians. They know what form of pesticides and pesticides to apply with a purpose to assist in killing and removing termites without harming people and the environment. But, it's far essential to pick out the proper business enterprise. The pest control company have to be certified by way of your nation. You can ask them to see the corporation's license and don't forget them hiring handiest if you discover them valid.

Say Goodbye to Termites with Professional Pest Control Services

Despite of your first-class efforts a few termites can go left out and will get an opportunity to preserve working on and harm your home. That's why you want professional's help so that you can do away with termites. Professional pest control technicians will look into your own home both interior and outdoors very well to check whether or not your house is invaded with termite or not. And if yes, then how intense the infestation is. After analyzing the property they may make a document on the circumstance of the property, severity of the infestation, and so forth. This report enables them growing the right pest control plan. Because then they'll realize what kind of remedy does it requires and additionally how lengthy it would take to cast off termites completely from your property.

Usually it's tough or almost not possible to dispose of termites in just one consultation. Termite control calls for distinct periods and this is the purpose why maximum of the termite control organizations provide termite manipulate service in programs. This manner you will best need to make one-time payment for all the periods. There are many pest control corporations that offer yearlong termite remedy safety for each business and home residences.

But, now what have to be bothering might without a doubt be the termite control fee. So, permit's discuss how a good deal does it value to avail termite control carrier.

Termite Control Cost

The average price for termite remedy ranges from Rs 1200 – Rs 9000. There are many stuff that are taken into consideration with the aid of the professional terminators to calculate the value of termite treatment. Most groups value as in keeping with square ft.

It manner the size of the vicinity is the primary factor that influences prices or price of termite manage carrier. Apart from this the severity of the infestation also performs an critical function.

The prices will growth if you'll preserve ignoring hiring expert exterminators or not rent the exterminators or the proper time. So, ebook your termite manipulate provider from a relied on and expert pest manipulate corporation in Delhi NCR and dispose of termites.

THE END

www.ingramcontent.com/pod-product-compliance
Lightning Source LLC
Chambersburg PA
CBHW060948130726
48001CB00003B/1115